THE SINGING DRUM

A Traditional Collection

THE SINGING DRUM

A Tale From Africa

THERE was once a young girl called Tselane who took her calabash to the river to fetch water. The calabash was made from a huge gourd, which took some filling, I can tell you. She dipped a small pitcher in and out of the water; dip, pour, dip, pour—and as she dipped and poured she sang. The song was so beautiful that all the animals near the river stopped drinking and came closer to listen to her song.

Hidden in the tall grass, not far from Tselane, a man with a drum sat and listened too. Well, he looked like a man, but he was in fact an ogre or *zimwi*, as the Bantu people call it.

3

So, just as Tselane had almost filled the calabash with water, the *zimwi* crept up behind her and pushed her into his drum, which was larger than she was.

Before she could utter a cry, the *zimwi* said, "Young girl, you sing very well. Now listen to me. When I beat this drum you must sing as well as you can, for as long as you can. If you do not sing, I will beat you instead of my drum."

Tselane was naturally rather afraid, so she agreed to do what he said. The *zimwi* picked up the drum with Tselane inside it and went away. When he came at last to a village, it was getting dark, so he asked the villagers if he could spend the night there. The chief agreed to let him stay and in payment for their hospitality, the *zimwi* said that he wished to play his drum to entertain the people.

As he beat the drum, Tselane began to sing. The villagers were delighted at the beautiful music. When at last she stopped singing, the people implored the *zimwi* to play the singing drum again. But the man answered, "I am hungry and tired, and I cannot play my drum again until I have eaten." When the people heard this, they were shocked at their thoughtlessness. They hurried to their gardens and filled their baskets with all the produce they could find—pumpkins, yams, red beans, and bananas. These they cooked and brought to the man, along with fresh goat's milk and sweet honey-beer. He ate and drank greedily until all the food was gone.

Then, "Boom! Boom!" Again he beat the drum and again Tselane began to sing, and she sang and sang and sang until the moon was high in the sky. Then she sang lullabies until all the villagers were nodding their heads sleepily and were dropping off to sleep one by one.

Then when everyone was fast asleep, the man opened the top of the drum and gave the girl five cold red beans, which had

dropped onto the ground while he gorged himself.

When morning came, the man went away with his drum to another village. The same thing happened as the night before, but this time the people cooked him a chicken stew which he devoured, leaving none at all for Tselane. From village to village he went, and wherever he went, the same thing happened.

People were astonished at the beautiful sounds which came from the singing drum, and whenever people heard him they fed him generously.

But did he share these good things with Tselane? Of course he

did no such thing! He only gave her enough to keep her voice from growing weak—four or five cold beans or a few pumpkin seeds.

When Tselane had failed to return to her own village, her parents had gone to the river to look for her. They found only the large calabash almost filled with water. Along the river's edge a crocodile blinked at them. They asked him if he had eaten their child, but he shook his head and swam away with a glint in his eyes. Sadly they wandered up the river from village to village, always searching and asking for news of their daughter. They grew weary and

ragged from their journeying from river to forest, from forest to plain; but Tselane could not be found.

One evening, hungry and exhausted, they stopped at a village and asked to spend the night there. The villagers welcomed them and told them that another stranger was also staying that night in the village, but there was still room for more. The other stranger was the man with the singing drum.

"Boom, Boom!" he beat the drum, and it began to sing. Tselane, hidden inside, sang about the things she had known and loved when she had lived outside in the sunshine…antelopes running through tall grasses…the gentle bleating of newborn kids…and the beauty of mountains reaching for the sky. She was sure that she would never see these things again, so she sang with longing which made her songs more haunting and tender than they had ever been before. The people listened with amazement, holding their breath so as not to miss a note.

Except for one. No sooner had Tselane begun to sing than her mother started to cry out, for she recognized the voice of her beloved daughter. But her father signaled to his wife to say nothing. For many hours the drum sang, and each song was more beautiful than the one before.

When the singing was done—for at last the man could play no longer until he had eaten—the people brought him the best foods they had and he ate greedily. "I am thirsty!" he cried, after he had devoured enough for ten men; and the people brought him calabashes and ostrich egg cups of sweet honey-beer. He drank and drank and drank, while Tselane's father sat beside him and flattered him about his wonderful drum and urged him to eat and drink some more. At last, when he had drunk enough for twenty men, he yawned loudly and fell asleep. All the people in the village went to their

9

houses to sleep, but Tselane's parents only pretended to sleep. When the drummer was snoring louder than a lion, they crept up to him. Quietly, quietly, they untied the thongs that held the drum skin to the drum and peeped inside. There was Tselane, their dear daughter, small and thin and frightened and lonely.

"Come out, come out," they whispered to her and held her tight.

Then her father lit the end of a stick in the fire and crept out into the forest.

Near an old tree he held the stick of fire, and after a moment swarms of bees emerged from a hole in the tree—for bees hate smoke, you know. As they swarmed around not knowing where to go, Tselane's father put the lighted stick close to them, and they flew ahead of him to escape the smoke. And so he drove them ahead of him, right back to the village of sleeping people and up to the *zimwi*'s empty drum.

Seeing the hole in the drum, the bees all flew in, and the father snapped the drum skin over the drum and smiled. Then the family went to sleep.

Morning came, and when everyone awoke, they begged the *zimwi* to play his drum again. No one noticed the strange young girl, for they could think of nothing but the beautiful songs of the night before.

"Please, please," they begged the man over and over again. "Play the drum for us before you go."

And the man rubbed his stomach and said, "I could play the drum quite well, if only I had a little breakfast!"

And the people then promised him that they would feast him with even more food than the night before and would shower him with many gifts besides, if he would only play one little short song before they went into their gardens to pick a feast for him—for there was nothing left in their houses.

And so the man agreed: one more song, that was all.

"Boom! Boom!"—he beat the drum, but nothing happened.

"Boom! Boom! Boom!"—angrily he pounded the drum again.

Nothing happened—but a few sniggers could be heard coming from the crowd.

"Boom! Boom! Boom! Boom!" Again and again he beat the drum, but nothing happened...nothing at all. By now all the people were laughing at him. He threw the drum on the ground and began to kick it and shout, but still the drum was silent.

At last, he picked up the drum and ran angrily out of the village, shouting as he ran, "I told you I would beat you if you did not sing— and now I *will*!"

So saying, he tore off the drum skin to beat Tselane, but—oh, my! Out came the bees...so many of them! "Bzzzzzzzzzzzzzzzz!" They flew after that man and chased him away, and no one ever saw or heard of him again.

As for Tselane, she sang her beautiful songs for the villagers before they went into their gardens for the day's work. They gave her good things to eat (for she was famished after being starved for so long) and many gifts of jewelry. Then the father and mother led their daughter out of the village and began their long journey home.

THE SORCERER'S APPRENTICE

A Story from Poland

 NCE a lad chanced to meet a tall man so stooped with age that he was as bent as the stick he leaned upon. "Where are you going, Boy?" the man asked.

"To seek my fortune," said the lad.

"Then, perhaps you could work for me. But first tell me, can you read?"

"Can I read? My Lord! I can read better than the schoolmaster, the doctor, and the village priest. Yes, I can!"

"Then, alas, you will be of no use to me," the old man said sadly, shuffling away, tortoise-slow and ruefully watched by the boy.

However, as soon as the old chap shuffled around the corner, the boy twirled around, jumped into the air, clicked his heels, snapped his fingers, and whooped. Almost before his feet hit the ground

again he was pulling off his jacket. One wriggle and a shove and a thrust and it was returned to his back, but inside out. *Slappity-Slap!* He brushed his hair down over his eyes, then raced off across the fields.

Some distance on, he rejoined the road, where he lolled by a tree to await the appearance of the old gentleman. Sure enough, he toddled into sight. "Good morning, Sir! Could you tell me if I could get work in these parts?" the boy called out in greeting.

"You could perhaps work for me. But first, young man, can you read?"

"Not a word!" lied the lad, hanging his head in regret.

"You're the lad I need," he was told. "Come along with me. It's good food that you'll have, a warm bed, and a silver shilling each week."

And so the boy took service with a Sorcerer, becoming his Apprentice.

Every day the Apprentice washed the flasks and scrubbed the caldron. He cleaned the shelves. He swept floors and sorted the herbs. He filled some bottles and emptied others. He dusted rows and rows of books, which he read whenever he was out of the Sorcerer's sight. It wasn't long before the hoodwinking young bluffer thought he knew as much about spells and magic as the Sorcerer had taken a lifetime to learn. If only he could test his skill... if only...if only!

The chance came on the day the Sorcerer said, "Amuse yourself this morning, Boy. I'll be away for an hour on business at the court."

Hurray! The Apprentice whistled with delight, and no sooner had the Sorcerer left than he was draping his birch broom in an old cloak Mutter-mutter-gibble-gabble! He chanted a spell. Presto! Marvello The broom became a man, a Broom-man with arms and legs like sticks and a shock of stiff ungroomed hair.

"Go to the well and fetch water for my bath," ordered the Apprentice.

"I obey!" rasped the Broom-man. He bent. He straightened, swinging a bucket in each hand. He marched straight-backed like a stake to the well. He drew water, stepped back to the house, and stalked down the stairs as stiff-legged as a crane from the marsh.

Water sploshed from the buckets to the bath. Then, up the stairs, out of the house, over the courtyard to the well stumped the Broom-man. Back to the bath! *Splash!* Back to the well! Back to the bath! *Splash!* Back to the well!

The Broom-man worked without a pause. He filled the bath to overflowing. Dribbling water puddled the floor. The puddle spread into a pool. Then the tiles were awash and a little stream trickled to the hall. "Stop! I told you to stop!"

The Broom-man worked on. In with full buckets! Out with empty buckets! In! Out! In! Out! "Stop! *Stop!*" screamed the Apprentice. Soon the Broom-Man was knee-deep in water, then thigh-deep, then waist-deep, then neck-deep in sloshing, rocking ice-cold water. Behind him gabbled the Apprentice repeating every spell he could remember. Each was useless.

He blocked the Broom-man's path. He stood astride with outstretched arms, but the Broom-man swung him aside, marched on, down the stairs, under the water to the bath.

In with full buckets! Out with empty buckets! In! Out! In! Out! Like a tide, the water rose up the stairs and flooded into the hall. Down the stairs, under the water continued the Broom-man. In! Out!

Miffed and flustered, the Apprentice grabbed the buckets as the Broom-man passed. He tugged. On strode the Broom-man dragging the Apprentice with him. Down the stairs! Under the water!

Spluttering, he released the buckets and, fuming with anger, the boy fetched an ax and rashly struck downward through the Broom-

man's head. It split in halves. Each piece became a new Broom-man. Each Broom-man carried two pails. Each bucket was filled with water. *Whack! Chip-chop! Chop-chop-chop!* The Apprentice split and gashed, surrounding himself with wood splinters. And up rose six, then twelve, twenty-four—a whole line of Broom-men filling and emptying buckets.

Water poured into the bedrooms, the kitchen, the Sorcerer's workshop. Half-swimming, half-wading, the frantic Apprentice fought the water to reach the shelves of great books and, with trembling fingers, he searched the pages for the right words to break the broom-stick spell.

All at once, large and fearsome, the Sorcerer stood in the doorway. The Apprentice slammed shut the book. The Sorcerer slammed the workshop door.

The boy stood there for a long time, hearing nothing except his beating heart, then the draining of water rushing and gurgling away. He believed he was imprisoned, but when he slunk to the door, it opened to his touch.

The water was gone, and only the broom's remains littered the tiles in a heap of snapped birch twigs and harmless splinters of wood. Two upturned buckets drained by the well, leaving a shallow puddle of water which soon dried in the sun.

There was no sign of the Sorcerer, so the Apprentice, with his hands in his pockets, swaggered down the road, whistling. Some say he later became a successful plumber and invented plug-holes with drains, a big improvement upon the Sorcerer's solid stone bath. And he was never to utter that charm, or any other as long as he lived. Never! He never knew how to undo the broom-stick spell. The Sorcerer had magicked away the great books, which was very prudent of him.

THAT WICKED CROW

An Australian Aboriginal Story

AH, that old crow! He was a bad one and no mistake. He flew about Australia looking for trouble, and if he couldn't find any, why, he just made some for himself.

None of the other birds liked him, and no wonder! They used to chase him away as soon as they set eyes on him, but then he started to call each one "brother-in-law." This was a trick to make them share their food with him, because relations must always share in Aboriginal families; and although they didn't think he really was their brother-in-law, they were not quite certain. So whichever bird it was—whether bower-bird or emu

or eagle—he usually let the crow get away with it. What if it really was his brother-in-law?

One day Crow flew to a part of the coast where he had never been before, and below him he saw a great flock of pelicans. Down drifted Crow, like a small black cloud bringing bad weather—or trouble of some kind, anyway—with him.

One of the pelicans looked up and blinked at him. "Greetings from me and my kinsmen, brother-in-law," said Crow.

"Those are strange words from a stranger," said the pelican. "I have never seen you before."

"It is a long story," said Crow. "In my country it is common

knowledge that we crows and you pelicans are related. A brother of my great-great grandfather married the sister of your grandmother's grand-aunt, and that, according to our laws, means that we are brothers and share all things in common. See! It is all written down here." And Crow held up a stick on which many signs had been cut.

The pelican had never learned to read, so he had no choice but to believe Crow. "Come along," he said. "Follow me and I will take you home." So the pelican hopped along and Crow followed, but he soon started to groan as if in pain and pretended to have a bad limp in one leg.

"What's the matter?"

"Oh, it is nothing," said Crow bravely and limped worse than ever. "It is just that on my way I got into a fight with a tribe of emus. Believe me, I gave as good as I got, but in the end the emu chief caught me off guard and stabbed me in the ankle with his spear. After that I had to fly for my life, or they would surely have torn me to pieces."

Crow could not tell the truth, try as hard as he liked— and he wasn't trying hard! But the pelican was impressed, and he helped Crow to reach the ground where the tribe was camped. All the pelicans gave him a friendly welcome, fed him with the best of their food, and then let him sleep in their favorite roosting place.

Crow slept deeply that night and well into the morning, for he was tired and his belly was full. When he awoke the sun was high. "What's this?" he said to himself. "I never sleep so late. That wretched pelican must have put a spell on me. I'll give him 'brother-in-law'! He will be sorry he played such a trick on me." And in no time at all, that crow had worked himself into a passion against the kind pelican.

Crow jumped up and looked about him. There was not a pelican in sight. There were tracks everywhere, however, and he followed them to a lagoon. The whole tribe was there, some of them fishing, some swimming, some just lying and gossiping on the banks, but all happy in the warm sun. Crow watched them, and the happier they became the more his hatred grew.

"How can I harm them most?" he muttered. He noticed that there were no babies in sight, so he poked around, looking for them. As he came to a tall gum tree, he heard

the sound of chirping and saw that the mothers had hidden their young in a fork, high enough to be safe from enemies.

"That's what I'll do!" said Crow. "I'll get those babies down and eat them all. They will make a tasty meal, and won't the mothers be upset? They will be sorry that they offended me. It will teach them not to tangle with Crow."

First he tried to fly up to the fork. When that failed he thought he would scramble up the trunk, but it was smooth as glass, and he just couldn't get a grip.

"Fine! I'll chop the tree down." He hurried back to the camp and stole an ax from the pelicans' shed. "Down it comes!" he shouted and swung the ax, but it twisted in his grip and nearly broke his wing.

"I'll burn it down." He took a torch and lit it at the camp fire, but when he put it to the tree, it just smoked and flickered and then went out.

"I know. I'll call up the forest spirits." So Crow began to sing an evil song. Out of the forest crept a crowd of tiny creatures which danced around the tree. "Grow, tree! Grow!" said Crow. Every time he said, "Grow," the spirits threw their boomerangs into the air and the tree grew upward. By the time Crow had finished his song, it was so tall that the baby birds and their refuge could scarcely be seen from the ground.

"That will serve those pelicans right!" gloated Crow, and he hid himself and waited to see what would happen.

Before long a carpet snake and his mate came to the foot of the tree. He had heard the noise made by the pelicans at their fishing and had decided that a few unguarded baby birds would do very well for dinner. But when he looked up, he realized that the birds were far beyond his reach.

Crow just couldn't keep quiet. "See what I did!" he boasted. "I showed those pelicans I am not to be trifled with. I forced the spirits to make the tree grow, and now nobody will ever get those babies down."

"You stupid bird!" hissed the snake. "It was bad enough wishing to hurt the pelicans who had done you no harm. Now you have done me out of my dinner, and that is far worse. If I get my coils around you, I'll teach you better manners!" And the snake and his mate wriggled away angrily into the forest.

By now the pelicans had finished their fishing, and the mothers came to collect their babies. What a commotion they made when they saw how high the tree had grown. They screamed and wailed until there was no animal for miles around that did not know of their troubles. From every side came kangaroos and goannas and possums and all the other beasts of forest and grassland, all swarming to the tree.

There were good climbers among them, but not one could reach those babies.

The blue wren, smallest of all birds, watched them for a time. Then he said to his wives, "Those great creatures are quite helpless. Wait here while I go and fetch the kookaburra bird." So he flew for miles through the woods until his little wings were weary, and at last he came upon the kookaburra.

"You are needed at the lagoon, old friend," said the wren. "Those poor clumsy pelicans are going to die of grief if nothing is done for them, and all the other animals are helpless. Follow me." And they flew back together.

Everyone was making too much noise to notice the two birds. "Fetch me the kangaroo," said the kookaburra, and the wren went and whispered in his ear, "The kookaburra wants a word with you. Come quietly."

The kookaburra told the kangaroo to get everyone to stand well back from the tree and shut their eyes. When every animal had obeyed, the kookaburra went to work. Without any fuss he flew up the tree, tied the first of the babies to his back with a strip of vine, and brought it safely to the ground. He repeated this until all the babies were tucked at the kangaroo's feet. Then the kookaburra flew back to his home in the forest with not a single word to anyone.

The kangaroo called out, "Open your eyes." Weren't those mothers pleased to see their babies sitting quietly on the ground? They rushed forward and nearly smothered them with kisses and cuddles. But when they remembered to thank the rescuer, he was not to be seen. He and his friend the wren wanted no fuss. Their pleasure was all in helping their neighbors without thought of reward.

As for Crow, when he saw his "brother-in-law" coming toward him with that great beak uplifted, he remembered that he had a job to do in a far-off part of Australia. Off he flew at top speed, and he took good care never to return to the pelicans' camping ground.

TWO OF EVERYTHING

A Story from China

M R. and Mrs. Hak Tak lived in a small house in a village high up in the mountains. They were rather old and rather poor, and the only land they had was a small steep patch on the mountainside. Here they grew vegetables, which were all they had to eat. If it was a good season and there were some left over, Mr. Hak Tak took what they could spare to the next village and sold them for what he could get—which was not much. Then he would buy some oil for their lamp, some fresh vegetable seeds, and sometimes (but not often)

some cotton material to make new clothes for himself and his wife. As you can imagine, they did not get the chance to eat meat or fish very often.

Now, one day a strange thing happened. Mr. Hak Tak was out digging in his precious patch of earth when he uncovered a large brass pot. How odd that he should not have noticed it before! Surely he had dug over all the earth many, many times before? He pulled it out and looked inside, but it was empty. Still, he thought that it might be useful; so when he had finished his digging in the evening, he decided to take it with him. It was very big and very heavy. As he struggled to get his arms around it and lift it up, his purse, which he always took with him in his belt, slipped onto the ground; so to keep it safe, he put it into the pot and staggered home with his load.

As soon as he got into the house, Mrs. Hak Tak hurried to meet him.

"My dear husband," she said. "Whatever have you got there?"

"For a cooking pot it is too large; for a bath it is too small," said Mr. Hak Tak, "but I found it buried in our vegetable patch and I have already found a use for it. I have used it to carry home my purse."

"Alas," said Mrs. Hak Tak, "something smaller would have done just as well to carry all the money we are ever likely to have," and she bent over the pot and peered into its dark inside.

As she bent over, her hairpin, which was made of carved bone and the only one she had, fell into the pot. She put her hand in to get it out again, and then she gave a loud cry. "What is it?" asked her husband in alarm. "Is there a viper in the pot?"

"Oh, my dear husband," she cried, "whatever is the meaning of this? I put my hand in the pot to get out my hairpin and your purse, and look, I have brought out two hairpins and two purses, each exactly like the other!"

"Open the purse. Open both purses," said Mr. Hak Tak. "One of them is sure to be empty."

But no. The second purse contained exactly the same amount of money as the first, and they couldn't tell the difference. Each looked exactly alike, and that meant, of course, that the Hak Taks now had exactly twice as much money as before.

"And two hairpins instead of one," said Mrs. Hak Tak, forgetting to pin up her hair in her excitement, so it fell streaming over her shoulders. "There is something very strange indeed about this pot."

"Let's put in a sack of lentils and see what happens," said Mr. Hak Tak.

They heaved in the bag of lentils—which was so big it almost filled the pot—and when they pulled it out again, there was another bag underneath exactly the same size, waiting to be pulled out also. So, of course, they now had two bags of lentils instead of one.

"Put in the blanket," said Mr. Hak Tak. "We need another blanket for the winter." And sure enough, when the blanket came out, there was another folded up behind it.

"Put in my padded coat," said Mr. Hak Tak, "then when winter comes there will be one for you as well as me. Let's put in everything that we have had to share. It's a pity that we don't have any meat or fish, because the pot can't seem to make anything without a pattern."

Then Mrs. Hak Tak, who was a most intelligent woman, said, "My dear husband, let's put in our purse again and again and again. If we take out two purses for every one we put in, we shall have enough money by tomorrow evening to buy everything we need."

"I'm afraid we may lose it this time," said Mr. Hak Tak, but in the end he agreed, and they threw in the purse and pulled out two. Then they added the new money to the old and threw it in again and pulled double the amount out.

After a while the floor was covered with old leather purses, and they decided just to throw the money in by itself. This worked well and saved trouble. Every time, twice as much money came out as went in, and every time they added the new coins to the old and threw them all in together. It took hours for them to tire

of this game, but at last Mrs. Hak Tak said, "My dear husband, there is no need for us to work so hard. We shall look after the pot so that it does not run away, and we can always make more money as we need it. Let's tie up what we have."

It made a huge bundle in the extra blanket, and the Hak Taks lay looking at it for a long time before they went to sleep, talking of all the things they would buy and the improvements they would make to their cottage.

The next morning they rose early. Mr. Hak Tak filled a purse with money from the bundle and set off for the village to buy more things in a single morning than he had bought in fifty whole years.

After Mrs. Hak Tak had seen him off, she cleaned up the cottage and put the rice on to boil. Then she took another look at the money and made herself a whole set of hairpins from the pot and about twenty candles instead of one, for that is all they had had up to then. Then she went to sleep for a while, since she had been up so late the night before, but just before her husband was due to come home, she awoke and went over to the pot. She dropped in a cabbage leaf to make sure it was still working properly, and when two leaves came out she sat down on the floor and put her arms around it.

"I do not know how or why you came to us, dear pot," she said, "but you are the best friend we ever had."

Then she knelt to look inside it. At that moment her husband came to the door, and, turning quickly to see all the wonderful things he had bought, she lost her balance and fell into the pot.

Mr. Hak Tak put his bundles down and ran across and caught her by the ankles and pulled her out but, oh, mercy! No sooner had he put her carefully down on the floor, than he saw the kicking legs of another Mrs. Hak Tak in the pot! What was he to do? He couldn't leave her there, so he caught her ankles and pulled, and another Mrs. Hak Tak, so exactly like the first that no one could have told them apart, stood beside them.

"What an extraordinary thing!" said Mr. Hak Tak, looking helplessly from one to the other.

"I won't have another Mrs. Hak Tak in the house," screamed the first Mrs. Hak Tak. Everything was in confusion. The first Mrs. Hak Tak wrung her hands and shouted and wept. Mr. Hak Tak was not much calmer, and the second Mrs. Hak Tak herself was so confused that she sat down on the floor as if she didn't know what would happen next.

"Now listen to me," said Mr. Hak Tak. "I want only one wife, but how could I have left her in the pot?"

"Put her back again at once," cried Mrs. Hak Tak.

"What! And pull two out?" said her husband. "If two wives are too many, what would I do with three? No! No! No!" He stepped back quickly as if he were stepping away from three wives, but he slipped and—you've guessed it—he fell into the pot!

Both Mrs. Hak Taks ran. They each caught an ankle and pulled him out and put him down on the floor but, of course, there was another pair of legs kicking in the pot. And soon a second Mr. Hak Tak, so exactly like the first that no one could have told the one from the other, stood beside them.

The first Mr. Hak Tak disliked the idea of a double as much as Mrs. Hak Tak had disliked hers. He shouted and raged and scolded his wife for pulling him out of the pot, while the second Mr. Hak Tak sat down on the floor beside the second Mrs. Hak Tak and looked as if, like her, he didn't know what would happen next.

The old Mrs. Hak Tak had a very good idea.

"Now listen, my dear husband," she said, "do stop shouting and listen. Don't you see that it is really a very good idea to have a new one of you as well as of me. For now we can go back to things as they were. We can settle down on our own, and these new people, who are ourselves yet not ourselves, can set up house next door to us!"

And that is what they did. The first Hak Taks used the money from the pot to build themselves a fine new house; then they built one exactly the same for the new couple. They all lived in great

harmony and friendliness because, as Mrs. Hak Tak said, "The new Mrs. Hak Tak is much more than a sister to me, and the new Mr. Hak Tak is much more than a brother to you!"

The neighbors were very surprised in the first place because of the sudden wealth and, secondly, because of the new couple who looked exactly like the old. They decided that they must be very close relations indeed, of whom they had never heard before. They said, "It looks as if after becoming so very rich, the Hak Taks have decided to have two of everything, including themselves, so that they can enjoy their money more."

NIX NOUGHT NOTHING

An Old German Story

ONCE, a King and Queen who had been long married were blessed with a son. At the time of the Prince's birth, the King was far away at a war, and his Queen did not name her baby. "We'll just call him Nix Nought Nothing until my Lord returns," she told the court. "The King must name his child." And strange as it sounds, Nix Nought Nothing he was called until he grew from baby to toddler, from toddler to noisy little boy.

By then, at long last, the King was returning home. His journey brought him to a river, which ran wide and wild in full flood. The King rode along the bank seeking a safe place to cross, but he found no shallows and the currents were too strong to swim his horse. He had to wait until the river fell.

As he dismounted, the ground shuddered. Then the trees swayed, shaking their boughs and shedding twigs. Above the river's roar grew a strange rumbling. It rumbled louder and closer until... until above the treetops a Giant grinned down on him. "What will you give me, King, if I carry you over the river?" he boomed.

The King, trying to conceal his shock, shouted back, "What is in my power to give you, Sir?"

"Awh! What about Nix Nought Nuttin'?"

"Come now! Nix Nought Nothing is too little payment for your service, Sir. I shall give you my thanks as well."

"Done!" droned the Giant. Little did the King know that he had unwittingly promised his small son to the Evil One.

With the King high on his shoulder, the Giant lurched across the river. "Don't forget! You promised me Nix Nought Nuttin'," he reminded the King, as he dumped His Majesty on the bank. "Should you forget, I will destroy your kingdom, your people, and you!" he threatened.

"I'll remember," nodded the King, believing the Giant was soft in the head. The Big Buffoon's threats were absurd moonshine twaddle, as foolish as his thick-skulled demand for Nix Nought Nothing. Pish and fiddle-de-dee!

Hours later the King's homecoming turned to sorrow and despair. His own son was Nix Nought Nothing! "What have I done?" he moaned. "What have I done?"

"Take heart! We shall *never* give our boy to the Giant," vowed the Queen.

Next morning, leering with malice, the Giant bent over the castle wall and bellowed for his reward. He was given a boy, the Henwife's lad, who was carried off, shoulder-high.

They jogged along and jogged along until they came to a rock which was large enough for the Giant to sit on, and as he eased out his long bulky legs, he asked, "Hidge-hodge on my back. What's the time now? Tell me that!"

"It's the time my mother takes the eggs to the castle fo the Queen's breakfast," piped up the Henwife's lad.

"*Arrrrh!*" The Giant was enraged. He dropped the boy. Roaring, thundering, punching at the air, he stamped back to the castle. "Give me Nix Nought Nuttin'!" he bellowed. And he was given a boy, the Gardener's lad, who was carried off, shoulder-high.

They trotted along and trotted along until they came to a rock which was large enough for the Giant to sit on. "Hidge-hodge on my back. What's the time now? Tell me that!" he rumbled.

"It's the time when my father cuts cabbages for the Queen's dinner," answered the Gardener's lad.

"*Orrrh!*" The Giant was livid. He dropped the lad. He raged. Pulling up trees, pitching rocks, kicking at hillsides, stomping on barns, he boiled back to the castle to shake its tower and thunder, "Trick me again, King-in-the-castle, and I will destroy your house, your people, your kingdom, and your Nix Nought Nuttin'."

Nix Nought Nothing yelled back, "Here I am, Giant. Take me!" And the Giant had him up on his back like a bag of chaff before the Queen could grab her child's coattails.

They traveled fast; traveled until the sun was setting and the Giant asked, "Hidge-hodge on my back. What's the time now? Tell me that!"

"It must be time for my father, the King, to sit at his supper," answered Nix Nought Nothing.

"Then the King has given me his promise," guffawed the Giant.

They traveled faster now, on to the Land of Giants where the Prince

was to grow from boy to man. During those years of imprisonment
his only friend was the Giant's daughter, and the Old Dunderhead
never realized how fond they were of each other. When at last he
realized that his Gillyflower and the Prince were friends, he fumed
and raged. He planned to be rid of the impertinent lickspittle of a
prince. "I've a stable seven miles long and seven miles wide. It's no
been cleaned for seven years. Clean it by sunset tomorrow or, Ni
Nought Nuttin', I'll have you for my supper."

The Prince surely would have been stewed or roasted if Gillyflower, small and fragile as her flower name, hadn't brewed a spell. Animals small and large from thereabouts flocked to her, and clouds of birds flew from the sky. "Please clean the stable before my Papa comes home!" she begged.

Animals scratched and dug and carried. Birds pecked and picked and carried. By sunset the stable was clean and the Giant purple with fury. "Shame on the clever one who has helped you!" he ranted. "And don't think I'm done with you yet. Tomorrow you will drain the castle's lake, or I'll eat you for supper, Nix Nought Nuttin'!"

The lake was seven miles long and seven miles wide and seven miles deep. Water lapped its shores, and, although the Prince worked digging drains and channels, the lake stayed brimful. It was a hopeless task until Gilly chanted a charm which brought the fish from the sea— flapping, slithering, flicking fish flying through the air. "Please drink the lake dry before my Papa comes home," begged Gilly.

Swallowing, gulping, gurgling fish drained the lake.

"Shame on the one who helped you!" raged the Giant. "And don't think I'm done with you yet. Tomorrow, Nix Nought Nuttin', you will bring me the egg from the nest that rests on the top of the pine trees, seven miles high. Otherwise I'll be eating you with bread and butter for supper."

Alas, Gilly knew no other spells or charms. There was only one way she could help the Prince. She used her fingers and toes as a ladder for Nix Nought Nothing to scale the tree. He took the egg, but as he slithered down it cracked inside his shirt.

"Somehow we must escape before Papa returns," said Gillyflower, and leaving the egg on the giant's table, she snatched up a magical flask which she clutched in both hands and they ran and they ran.

Too soon the Giant pursued them, his long earth-rocking strides bringing him close.

"Take the pin from my hair," Gilly told Nix Nought Nothing. "Cast it down behind us."

The Prince threw down the pin and wonders upon wonders, a river flowed between them and the Giant!

They ran farther, but too soon the Giant crossed the river. Too soon, they heard his pounding feet.

"Take the comb from my hair and cast it behind us," Gilly cried out.

Nix Nought Nothing threw down the comb. At once a hedge bristling with thorns, sprang up between them and the Giant.

They ran much farther, but too soon the Giant plunged through the hedge and too soon, his heavy breathing was like a hot wind on their backs.

Gilly turned. She threw down the flask. It broke into a hundred

gleaming crystals of diamond-bright glass, and from the crystals rose a foaming water wave which arched over the Giant, engulfing him, swirling him, drowning him.

Gilly, shocked and exhausted, could not travel on. Nix Nought Nothing went ahead alone to find them shelter. Soon he came to a castle standing behind walls of a great height, and there, tired to his very bones, the Prince fell wearily asleep in a chair near the door to the great hall.

The castle folk gathered about him, inspecting and guessing that he could only be a foreign prince. And the Gardener's daughter sidled up to peep and admire. She was vastly annoyed when the Cook sent her to fetch water from the well.

By this time Gilly had entered the castle grounds. She heard the stomping footsteps and the clanking bucket as the girl neared the well. Gilly fled into the nearby tree, clinging to a bough, fearful that the angry girl would discover her refuge.

The Gardener's daughter did glimpse Gilly's reflection. Her pale face, framed in leaves, shone as if from a mirror in the water below her. "Glory be!" sighed the Gardener's daughter. "It's lovely and beautiful I am, and I never did know it!" She dropped her bucket.

"What am I, a lovely-lovely, doin' here at the well? I'll go up to the castle and marry that Prince." She flounced away, tripping lightly with toes turned out and her nose tipped up in the air.

The Gardener discovered his daughter in her conceited state when the Cook shouted for water, so he went to the well himself. He, too, gazed upon Gilly's reflection. "Hey, you! Come down from there!" he ordered her. "*You*, rickety old hag, have bewitched my daughter!"

Gilly scrambled from the tree, and the Gardener saw that she was a frightened weary girl, trying hard not to weep. "Now then, a tree's no place for a lady, Ma'am!" he said, offering her his arm. "I'll take you to the Queen."

As they entered the castle hall Gilly pulled away to fling herself at the Prince's feet. "Wake! Speak to me!" she whispered, taking his hands and kissing them, wetting them with her tears.

The castle folk gawked, then shuffled aside unwillingly to admit the Queen, and then the King, who heard Gillyflower sob,

"I cleared the stable,
I drained the lake,
I climbed the tree
For love of thee.
Wilt thou now awake
And speak to me?
Speak to me!"

She pressed his hands against her cheek and looked at the Queen in anguish. "Nix Nought Nothing cannot speak to me."

"Nix Nought Nothing!" repeated the Queen faintly, pale and astonished.

"*My son*!" shouted the King, clutching the Queen.

They thrust Gilly aside. The Queen snatched Nix Nought Nothing into her arms and rocked him. He woke bewildered, looking about wildly, struggling to escape, until his eyes met Gilly's and he smiled with joy.

It was a long time before the excitement simmered down and stories were exchanged. There was never any doubt that Nix Nought Nothing was safely home. The grateful King and elated Queen wanted nothing more than Gillyflower to live with them as their daughter.

Nix Nought Nothing wanted nothing more than for Gilly to marry him, which she did in due course, and everyone lived happily for the rest of their lives.

HOW THE FOX CAME TO BE WHERE IT IS

OW there were two creatures that were very much alike. Only one was rusty-red with a thick tail, neat legs, and black-tipped ears, while the other was just plain shaggy black-and-white. They were both rivals for the job of guarding Man's farm from the other animals.

The shaggy black-and-white one was called Foursquare, and he wanted the job because he longed to lie beside Man's fire on the cold nights. The rusty-red one was called Slylooking, and he wanted the job for a very different reason. He loved cabbages, and the only way to get near Man's cabbages was by pretending to guard them.

This rivalry went on for a long time, and still neither of them had gotten the job. At last Man told them to settle the matter between themselves within a week, or else he would have to employ a bird.

"It is plain," said Slylooking, "that we must put our problem before the committee."

"Very well," said Foursquare. "Glad to see you so fairminded. I suggest that we let the cows decide it. They ponder a great deal."

"But about what?" cried Slylooking, pretending to be alarmed. "Scenery! That's what they ponder about. They gaze at the scenery and it looks as if they're pondering and so they get a great name as thinkers. They're no use for important, deep problems such as ours."

"Then whom do you suggest?"

Now Slylooking had a secret plan. "I suggest," he said with a sly look, "I suggest the hens. They sit on their perches without moving, and in the dark and all night long they have nothing else to do but think. They have no scenery to distract them. Besides, they have a fine chairman, the rooster, who keeps them in very good order."

"Then hens it is," said Foursquare generously. The hens listened carefully to the problem and promised to give their answer by eleven o'clock the next morning.

Foursquare found a soft warm place between hayricks and settled down for the night. But Slylooking could not sleep. He had much too much to do.

First of all he went to Rabbit-Becomer. He said that he had discovered a whole store of cabbages, which he knew Rabbit loved as much as he himself did.

"Where? Where?" cried Rabbit, hopping from one leg to the other.

"Well," said Slylooking with a sly look, "they're in the garden inside Man's farm. If only I could dig a hole as well as you can, I'd have them in a jiffy. Now if you…"

His voice sank to a whisper.

Away went Rabbit with Slylooking to dig the hole. After an hour's hard digging under Slylooking's directions, Rabbit burst up through the floor of the henhouse. In a flash, Slylooking slipped past him. The hens shouted and flapped in the darkness for a moment— then snickity-snackity! Fox had gobbled the lot.

"These are lively cabbages," said Rabbit, blinking in the darkness.

"They're the wrong ones!" cried Slylooking, pretending to be very alarmed. "Run for your life, they don't taste like cabbages at all. I think they're roosters and hens."

At this, Rabbit ran, and behind him, laughing silently, ran Slylooking, away down the long burrow.

Next morning Slylooking roused Foursquare, and together they went along to the henhouse to hear the decision. Slylooking kept his head turned so that Foursquare would not see him smile. He knocked loudly on the henhouse door. When there was no answer, he pretended to look very surprised.

"They must be still deep in thought," he said, as he knocked again. Still there was no answer, and with a puzzled frown at Foursquare, he opened the door and immediately jumped back.

"Murder! Murder!" he cried. "Oh, look at the poor hens!"

Foursquare ran in. Nothing was to be seen but piles of feathers and a fresh rabbit hole in the middle of the floor.

"Who's been here?" cried Slylooking, pointing at the burrow.

"Well, that looks like Rabbit's work," said Foursquare.

"The villain!" cried Slylooking. "Does he hope to get away with this?"

And away he went down the long burrow, almost choking with laughter.

He found Rabbit crouched in the end of a side-shoot, still trembling, terrified by what Slylooking had persuaded him to do. Without a word, Slylooking bundled him into a sack and carried him back to Man.

"Here's the villain who murdered all your poor chickens," he said. "Put him in your pot."

Man was delighted. He was so pleased, in fact, that he employed Slylooking on the spot to guard his farm and told him to go and tell Foursquare the decision.

And so Slylooking became the sentry at the farm and was happy among the cabbages. But not for long. He could not get out of his head the way those hens had tasted. One night as he patrolled the farm, chewing a cabbage leaf, he thought and thought of those hens until he could bear it no longer. There were new hens in the henhouse, and Slylooking went straight there.

"Good evening, ladies," he said as he entered. "Is everything all right?" Once he had the door closed behind him, he chose the fattest hen and snap! She was gone. The others looked at him in alarm.

"What will Man say when we tell him?" they cried.

Slylooking smiled, and snuppity, snippity, snoppity, snap! There was nothing left but a pile of feathers.

Next morning, Man just couldn't understand it. But he put new hens in the henhouse. Slylooking swore he had never heard a thing.

That night he visited the henhouse again.

And so every night for a week. He couldn't resist it. And each

54

time he had to gobble up every single hen lest any be left to tell Man what he had been up to. He completely lost his taste for cabbage leaves.

One evening, as he was going for a stroll in the fields, he met Foursquare.

"What are you doing, still snooping around here? Away with you!" he cried. "I'm to guard the farm against such creatures as you."

Foursquare looked at him steadily and said, "You have a hen feather in the corner of your mouth."

Slylooking was furious, but before he could say anything Foursquare had walked away.

Slylooking didn't like Foursquare's remark at all. It looked as if he suspected the truth. So Slylooking decided to play a trick on Foursquare and get rid of him. He went straight to Man.

"I have an idea," he said, with a sly look, "that Foursquare is at the bottom of this hen mystery. He is taking his revenge on you for employing me instead of him."

"Why," said Man, "that seems very likely. Certainly he has very fierce teeth. But how are we to catch him?"

"Leave it to me," said Slylooking. He had another plan already worked out.

Away he went, and finally he found Foursquare sitting on a green hill watching the river.

"Someone is still eating Man's hens," said Slylooking. "Will you help us to catch him?"

Now Foursquare was a very honest creature, and when he heard this he was quite ready to believe that Slylooking was not the culprit as he had suspected.

"How are we to do it?" he asked.

"Well," said Slylooking, "it isn't clear whether the murderer comes up through the floor of the henhouse, or whether he comes over the farmyard gate and in at the henhouse door. So tonight, while I watch the farm gate, I want you to hide in the henhouse and keep an eye on the floor."

"Well, that should catch him, whoever it is," said Foursquare. "What time shall I come?"

"Come about midnight. I'll let you in," said Slylooking with a sly look.

A quarter of an hour before midnight, Slylooking slipped into the henhouse and had a banquet of hens. Then he went off to meet Foursquare. Foursquare was waiting under the hedge.

"Quickly, quickly!" said Slylooking. "The murderer may be here any minute. Hurry. Into the henhouse."

As soon as Foursquare was in the henhouse with the pile of feathers, Slylooking bolted the door and ran for Man.

"I've trapped the murderer!" he cried. "I've got him!"

Man came running to see who it was.

"Why, it's Foursquare. Just as you said. Well done, Slylooking." Man dragged Foursquare out of the henhouse, tied him to the fence, and ran to fetch his gun.

Slylooking danced around poor Foursquare, looking at him merrily out of the corner of his eye and singing:

This is the end of this stor-ee,
Bullets for you and chickens for me.

"Oh, is that so!" roared Man's voice. He had returned more quickly than Slylooking had expected. Bang! went his gun, and Bang! But Slylooking was over the wall and three fields away and still running.

Then and there Man untied Foursquare and led him into the farm kitchen. He gave him a great bowlful of food and after that a rug to stretch out on by the fireside.

But that night, and every night after it, Slylooking had to sleep in the wet woods. And whenever he came sneaking back to the farm, sniffing for hens, Foursquare would hear him. He would jump up from his rug, barking at the top of his voice, and Man would be out through the door with his gun.

But Slylooking was too foxy to be caught. In fact, he was so foxy that pretty soon nobody called him Slylooking any more. They called him what we call him—just plain Fox.